HOLLYWOOD
DOGS

E D I T E D   B Y   J . C .   S U A R È S

CollinsPublishersSanFrancisco
A Division of HarperCollins*Publishers*

First published 1993 by Collins Publishers San Francisco

Copyright © 1993 J.C. Suarès

Captions copyright © 1993 Jane R. Martin

Additional copyright information page 80

Picture Research and Permissions: S.D. Evans

Library of Congress Cataloging-in-Publication Data

Hollywood dogs/edited by J.C. Suarès

p.   cm.

ISBN 0-00-255249-3

1. Dogs in motion pictures--Pictorial works. 2. Motion picture actors and actresses--
Pictorial works. I. Suarès, Jean-Claude.

PN1995.9.A5H65 1993

791.43'66--dc20   93-18219 CIP

LOVE CRAZY. 1941
*Head stuck between the elevator doors, William Powell is at the
mercy of the terrier in this romantic comedy with Myrna Loy.*

The first dog movie star was Rin Tin Tin, a German Shepherd. So popular were his movies that German Shepherds became the most popular breed in the world and Rin Tin Tin, the most famous dog. His first feature-length picture, *The Night Cry*, a silent production, opened to rave reviews in 1926. It was followed by several talkies, including *The Lone Defender* (1930), *The Lightning Warrior* (1931) and *The Wolf Dog* (1933), Rin Tin Tin's last picture. Rin Tin Tin Jr. went on to star in his own movies, including *The Law of the Wild* (1934) and *The Adventures of Rex and Rinty* (1935).

What Rin Tin Tin did for German Shepherds was matched only by what the great Lassie did for Collies. In a half-dozen technicolor adventures starting with *Lassie Come Home* in 1943, Lassie joined the RAF, beat the Nazis, helped liberate Norway and, despite several bullet wounds, managed to end up in the arms of a young Elizabeth Taylor.

In peacetime, Lassie enjoyed a long television run. The last Lassie movie, *The Magic of Lassie*, was released in 1978. There have been dozens of dog movies in the past four decades. But despite isolated successes such as *Old Yeller* (1957), *Dog of Flanders* (1959), *The Shaggy Dog* (1959), *Lad, A Dog* (1962), *The Ugly Dachshund* (1966), *Benji* (1974) and *The Shaggy D.A.* (1976), it has only been recently that Hollywood has gone on another dog movie binge. Blame it all on *Beethoven* (1992). The Universal production cost a mere $8 million, but went on to gross $60 million in North American box offices alone, making its star, a big sloppy St. Bernard, a household name.

Until then, dog movies had gone the way of musicals and westerns: nobody made them because the form seemed to have run its course. But *Beethoven* changed all that, and at last count there were half a dozen productions in the works. Among them is *Cyrano*, a 20th Century Fox production about a police dog who initiates so many mob arrests that a contract is put out on him. He is relocated to surburbia with a typical American family where he is quick to sniff out the teenagers' dope stash. New Line Cinema is developing *Man's Best Friend*, about a canine Robocop-like creature, half-dog and half-machine, while Warner Brothers and Disney are collaborating on *The Trial of King Boots*, the true story of a dog's trial for murder. Also in the works is *Ace Ventura, Pet Detective* (WB). And, of course, Universal is planning a sequel to *Beethoven*.

Despite the ups and downs in the number of full-length dog pictures, dogs have always enjoyed some of the juiciest supporting roles in Hollywood. What would the *Thin Man* series be without Asta? Or *Blondie* without Daisy? Or *Little Orphan Annie* without Sandy?

But the greatest of all dog supporting roles came in the form of a fifteen-pound Cairn Terrier named Terry, who played Toto to Judy Garland's Dorothy and Margaret Hamilton's Miss Gulch (also the Wicked Witch of the West) in the great 1939 classic, *The Wizard of Oz*. Terry was a timid dog who preferred to hide under a chair rather than confront the monster wind machines on the set. During one rehearsal, he was stepped on by an extra and was out of commission for three weeks. For all this he earned only $125 per week, making him the lowest paid performer in the cast (second lowest was Judy Garland at $500 per week. Bert Lahr, the Cowardly Lion, got $2,500). Despite the setbacks, Terry put in a brilliant performance and became a star, causing the public to rush to pet shops for Cairn Terriers. He never teamed up with *la* Garland again but co-starred with Miss Hamilton in the romantic comedy *Twin Beds* three years later.

J.C. Suarès

BETTE DAVIS AND MEG, 1930s
Warner Brothers distributed this still for The Adopted Father.
*Davis is shown with "Meg, her little Scottie who makes his
film debut with his mistress…His name is 'Meg' because he
isn't a crooner."*

LIMBURGER
BOMBS

FLEA
GRENADES

DOGS IN THE TRENCHES.
1930s
*Dogs brave WWI trenches in
the* Bugsy Malone *of dog
movies.*

11

RENNIE RENFRO AND BUSTER. 1930S
Above: *MGM's famous animal trainer gives the indomitable
star of the "Barkies" a reading lesson.*

THE CALLAHANS AND THE MURPHYS. 1927
Right: *MGM's comedy about feuding Irish families culminated
in a St. Patrick's Day picnic free-for-all. Directed by George
W. Hill, it starred Marie Dressler and Polly Moran. The dog,
pictured here with Sally O'Neil, was trained to sit up and
cover its ears.*

MGM-7733

14

VALENTINO. 1977
Carol Kane, as a Hollywood
starlet who befriends Valentino,
poses next to her Silver Ghost
with an elegant brace of
Borzois. Imported in very small
numbers to the United States
at the turn of the century,
Borzois were much in vogue in
the 1920s.

AILEEN QUINN AND SANDY. 1982
Above: *The orphan and her dog are the stars of Columbia
Pictures' version of* Annie, *directed by John Huston.*

THE STOWAWAY. 1936
Left: *Curly-topped, tiny Shirley Temple played a talented waif
orphaned in China who is befriended by this curly-topped,
tiny mutt.*

SOPHIA LOREN AND LABRADOR PUPPIES. 1963
La *Loren, star of* The Condemned of Altona *directed by Vittorio De Sica, plays with a litter of Labs.*

THE LITTLE RASCALS. 1920s
Previous pages: *Pete the Pup, a Pit Bull mix, had a fresh circle
drawn around his eye for every shoot.*

MAUREEN O'SULLIVAN AND JUNIOR. 1933
Right: *As an MGM featured player, O'Sullivan gives her Toy
Fox Terrier puppy some water. She starred in the dramatic
comedy,* Tugboat Annie, *and later played Jane to Johnny
Weissmuller's Tarzan.*

HUMPHREY BOGART WITH SCOTTISH TERRIERS,
1940s
The star of To Have and Have Not *looks over his gun collection
at home, accompanied by his watchful Scotties.*

AFTER THE THIN MAN, 1936
Three-way chemistry gave the series consistent appeal. Asta
the Fox Terrier leads the way for William Powell and Myrna
Loy on the search for a midnight snack.

RIN TIN TIN. 1920s
Above: *Audrey Ferris plays ball with Hollywood's foremost
German Shepherd.*

JOAN CRAWFORD AND DOUGLAS FAIRBANKS, JR.
WITH BOXER. 1929
Right: *A honeymoon photograph of Hollywood royalty
at Catalina Beach. Crawford was fresh from filming*

EVA GABOR. 1956
The future star of Green Acres *poses with her Poodle and West Highland White Terrier in her Los Angeles backyard.*

THE CALL OF THE WILD, 1935

*Above and right: Clark Gable's co-star was a St. Bernard
named Buck. The precocious giant made his trainer, Carl
Spitz, famous. Four years later Spitz was called upon for
The Wizard of Oz.*

BING CROSBY. 1930s
Above: *In dandy white trousers and slicked-back hair,
the young crooner from* Anything Goes *poses with his
German Shepherd.*

DOUGLAS FAIRBANKS, SR. 1920s
Right: *The matinee idol from* The Mark of Zorro *and*
The Thief of Bagdad *strikes an animated pose with his bat-
eared French Bulldog. The breed, with its compact, jaunty
elegance and highly refined pedigree, was popular among
stars of the day.*

AX-103-44

37

Peter Lawford holds an impeccably groomed Collie still as they
hide from a patrolling Nazi guard.

KATHARINE HEPBURN. 1930S
*Another mark of the well-bred, sporting life: a young
Hepburn, who débuted in* A Bill of Divorcement, *with
English Springer Spaniels.*

K-9. 1989
Previous Pages: *James Belushi's tougher partner, Jerry Lee,
rides shotgun in the Mustang. The black and tan German
Shepherd was trained by Hollywood animal pros
Karl Lewis Miller and Teresa Ann Miller.*

SIX OF A KIND. 1934
Right: *George Burns, Gracie Allen, and a Great Dane in this
zany comedy about traveling west, directed by Leo McCarey.*

DOUGHBOYS. 1930
Above: *Buster Keaton is an inept soldier whose only friend is a sympathetic mutt.*

PATTON. 1970
Right: *A stocky Bull Terrier stands next to George C. Scott. In the movie the dog turned out to be a coward, much to Patton's chagrin.*

THE WIZARD OF OZ. 1939

Terry, the Cairn Terrier who played Toto, was the lowest-paid and, according to her trainer Carl Spitz, the hardest working of the principal cast. During the production, it took Terry weeks to overcome her fear of the wind machines. She finally learned to duck behind Garland and Bolger.

AIR RAID WARDENS. 1943
In a typically impossible gag, Stan Laurel and Oliver Hardy
try to hush their whining mutt during a solemn meeting.
During the silents, trainers could teach a dog to whine to
spoken cues. With the advent of the talkies, they had to resort
to hand signals.

JAYNE MANSFIELD AND PEKINGESE. 1960
Rained out from filming Too Hot to Handle, *Jayne Mansfield poses with Powder Puff.*

THE HOUND OF THE BASKERVILLES. 1939
Richard Greene is attacked by the dreaded hound in this
version of Conan Doyle's classic tale, directed by
Sidney Lanfield and released by 20th Century Fox. The dog
used here, a Great Dane, is lighter than the Mastiff
Conan Doyle described.

BLONDIE, 1938
Columbia Pictures brought Blondie, *Chic Young's comic strip,
to the screen. Penny Singleton played Blondie, Arthur Lake
played Dagwood, Larry Simms was Baby Dumpling, and
Spooks was Daisy the Pup.*

JEAN HARLOW. 1932
MGM's blonde bombshell poses with a pair of Old English Sheepdogs.

KELLY AND ME. 1957
Above: *Man's best friend comes through again—in this case by partnering Van Johnson as a hoofer whose career is boosted to the bigtime. The white German Shepherd was touted as "an amazing canine star."*

WILLIAM POWELL AND HIS DACHSHUND. 1941
Left: *The star of MGM's* Love Crazy *runs his dog Fritzie through his paces.*

GOODBYE, MY LADY, 1956
William Wellman directed Walter Brennan and Brandon de
Wilde in the screen version of James Street's novel. The story,
about a boy and a remarkable dog who cleans herself like a
cat and never barks, starred an African Basenji.

A DOG OF FLANDERS. 1935
An RKO heartwarmer about a boy and his dog directed by
Edward Sloman, with Frankie Thomas, Helen Parrish, Richard
Quine, and Lightning the pup.

JEAN HARLOW. 1933
The star beams in the sun, holding a Wire-haired Fox Terrier.

THE ACCIDENTAL TOURIST. 1988
William Hurt is exasperated by Edward, his Cardigan Welsh
Corgi, in Warner Brothers' screen adaptation of the bestseller
by Anne Tyler. Geena Davis played the trainer who finally
reforms the incorrigible Edward. The dog's real trainers were
Boone Narr and Dave McMillan.

WON TON TON, THE DOG WHO SAVED
HOLLYWOOD. 1976
*Madeline Kahn starred with a German Shepherd, Teri Garr,
and Bruce Dern in this spoof of movie-making in the 1920s.*

JOAN CRAWFORD AT HOME WITH HER
DACHSHUNDS. 1940s
The star of Mildred Pierce *is greeted by her dog at poolside.*
Dachshunds—tidy, expressive, and loyal—were favorites
during Hollywood's golden years.

LASSIE COME HOME, 1943
In the first of the successful series, Lassie—played by Pal the Collie—paws at her sleeping master—played by Roddy McDowall. The movie, in which Lassie crosses the country to return to her owners, forever linked Collies with heroic loyalty.

IT'S A DOG'S LIFE. 1955
Left and above: *The rags-to-riches-tale was narrated by its
own star, a Bull Terrier named Windfire. Officially known as
Cadence Glacier, C.D.X., the dog was a show champion for
owners Lillian Ritchell and Claudia Stack. He won the
American Humane Association's 6th Annual Patsy award in
1956 for trainer William Koehler. Koehler, the chief trainer for
Walt Disney Studios in the 50s, also trained Sam, the star of*
The Shaggy Dog, *and the Fox Terrier who played Asta in
television's version of* The Thin Man.

COURAGE OF LASSIE. 1946

*When Lassie is forced into duty as a canine killer during World
War II, it takes the tender patience of young Elizabeth Taylor to
turn her back into a family dog. As a child star in Hollywood,
Taylor owned an English Springer Spaniel and a Golden
Retriever, as well as seven chipmunks and a cat named Jill.*

RICHARD BURTON AND ELIZABETH TAYLOR, 1971
*While in London, the stars stayed on their boat on the Thames
for the entire duration of their visit to avoid subjecting their
Lhasa Apsos and Pekingese to a six-month quarantine.*

BENJI AND COUGAR. 1987
*Walt Disney's Benji series made the mutt, trained by Frank
Inn, a box office star. Among the co-stars in this installment,*
Benji the Hunted, *were a golden eagle, a timber wolf, a Kodiak
bear and a mountain lion, handled by Working Wildlife, Inc.*

Photographic Acknowledgments

Cover: *Archive Photos*
3: *Everett Collection*
9: *Everett Collection*
10-11: *Culver Pictures*
12: *Culver Pictures*
13: *Culver Pictures*
15: *Neal Peters Collection*
16-17: *Everett Collection*
18: *Photofest*
19: *Photofest*
21: *Courtesy The Kobal Collection*
22-23: *Culver Pictures*
25: *Culver Pictures*
27: *Courtesy Motion Picture &
    Television Photo Archive*
29: *Courtesy The Kobal Collection*
30: *Culver Pictures*
31: *Courtesy The Kobal Collection*
33: *Photo by © Richard Miller/Motion
    Picture & Television Photo Archive*
34: *Everett Collection*
35: *Culver Pictures*
36: *Archive Photos*
37: *Photofest*
39: *Courtesy The Kobal Collection*
41: *Courtesy Motion Picture &
    Television Photo Archive*
42-43: *Archive Photos*

45: *Archive Photos*
46: *Courtesy The Kobal Collection*
47: *Photofest*
48: *Culver Pictures*
49: *Everett Collection*
51: *Archive Photos*
52: *Everett Collection*
55: *Photofest*
56: *Everett Collection*
57: *Photofest*
59: *Culver Pictures*
60: *Everett Collection*
61: *Culver Pictures*
63: *Photofest*
64: *Courtesy The Kobal Collection*
65: *Culver Pictures*
67: *Photofest*
68: *Culver Pictures*
69: *Archive Photos*
71: *Archive Photos*
73: *Archive Photos*
74: *Everett Collection*
75: *Everett Collection*
76: *Courtesy The Kobal Collection*
77: *Archive Photos*
78: *Archive Photos*
Back Cover: *Courtesy The Kobal
    Collection*